THE

of CONTENTS

Dear friend,

Did you know that God is thrilled to hear you pray the Prayer of Jabez? He longs to answer your prayers! Why *wouldn't* He want to pour out His blessings on you? Why *wouldn't* He want to give you more to do for Him? Why *wouldn't* He want to put His hand on you and fill you with His Spirit? Why *wouldn't* He want to keep you from evil so that you won't grieve His Holy Spirit?

I hope you will join me and many other women in this exciting journey as we dig deeper into God's Word. Allow these four principles of prayer from 1 Corinthians 4:10 to transform your relationship to God. And may God work in your life that you will say from experience, "He truly loves to pour out His blessings on us!"

Darlene

Darlene Wilkinson
Author, *The Prayer of Jabez for Women*

BLESS ME INDEED!

Introduction

And Jabez called on the God of Israel saying, "Oh, that You would bless me indeed, and enlarge my territory, that Your hand would be with me, and that You would keep me from evil, that I may not cause pain!" So God granted him what he requested. 1 Chronicles 4:10

I. The Mindset

And Jabez called on the God of Israel saying, " Oh, that you would bless me indeed!" So God granted him what he requested. I Chronicles 4:10

A. God blesses you on the basis of His

G _____.

For You, Lord, are good and ready to forgive, and abundant in mercy to all those who call upon You. Psalm 86:5

The Lord is merciful and gracious, slow to anger and abounding in mercy. Psalm 103:8

B. God does not bless you on the basis of your

G_____.

He has not dealt with us according to our sins, nor
punished us according to our iniquities, for as the heavens
are high above the earth, so great is His mercy toward
those who fear Him.   Psalm 103:10-11

Call to Me, and I will answer you, and show you great and
mighty things, which you do not know.   Colossians 4:2

II. The Message

A. God's blessing will create a lifestyle of

S _____.

Then Mary said, "Behold the maidservant of the Lord!
Let it be to me according to your word." And the angel
departed from her. And Mary said, "My soul magnifies the
Lord, and my spirit has rejoiced in God my Savior. For He
has regarded the lowly state of His maidservant; For
behold, henceforth all generations will call me blessed. For
He who is mighty has done great things for me, and holy
is His name.   Luke 1:38, 46-49

B. God's blessing will complete your search for

S _____.

In those days, while Mordecai sat within the king's gate,
two of the king's eunuchs, Bigthan and Teresh, doorkeepers,
became furious and sought to lay hands on King
Ahasuerus. So the matter became known to Mordecai, who
told Queen Esther, and Esther informed the king in
Mordecai's name.   Esther 2:21-22

C. God's blessing will convince you of His

S _____.

So it came to pass in the process of time that Hannah conceived and bore a son, and called his name Samuel, saying, "Because I have asked for him from the Lord." For this child I prayed, and the Lord has granted me my petition which I asked of Him. 1 Samuel 1:20, 27, 28

III. The Method

A. Ask for God's blessing

P_____.

Therefore I say to you, whatever things you ask when you pray, believe that you receive them, and you will have them. Mark 11:24

Continue earnestly in prayer, being vigilant in it with thanksgiving. Colossians 4:2

B. Acknowledge God's blessing

P _____.

Return to your own house, and tell what great things God has done for you. Luke 8:39

Every good gift and every perfect gift is from above, and comes down from the Father of lights, with whom there is no variation or shadow of turning. James 1:17

CONCLUSION

Now to Him who is able to do exceedingly abundantly above all that we ask or think, according to the power that works in us, to Him be glory in the church by Christ Jesus throughout all ages, world without end. Amen. Ephesians 3:20

BLESS ME INDEED!

1. How does a woman's childhood and her relationship to her father affect her view of God? How will that view of God affect the way she prays?

2. Read Psalm 86:5 and discuss how to have this mindset about God's character. Share other verses that talk about God's willingness to give (i.e. Luke 11:13, James 1:17, etc.).

3. How do women search for significance differently than men? According to Jeremiah 9:23-24, what does God consider significant? How does "being blessed" by God affect your sense of significance?

4. How does praying for and receiving a blessing enable you to know and understand God better? How does this determine the intensity of your prayers?

Enlarge My Territory!

Introduction

And Jabez called on the God of Israel saying, "Oh, that You would bless me indeed, and enlarge my territory, that Your hand would be with me, and that You would keep me from evil, that I may not cause pain!" So God granted him what he requested.   1 Chronicles 4:10

I. The Mindset

And Jabez called on the God of Israel saying, "Oh that You would enlarge my territory!" So God granted him what he requested.   1 Chronicles 4:10

A. God will enlarge your territory and require you to relinquish C _____.

The sacrifices of God are a broken spirit, A broken and a contrite heart – these, O God, You will not despise.
Psalm 51:17

"Most assuredly, I say to you, unless a grain of wheat falls into the ground and dies, it remains alone; but if it dies it produces much grain. He who loves his life will lose it, and he who hates his life in this world will keep it for eternal life.   John 12:24-25

B. God will enlarge your territory and require you to make a C _____.

And if it seems evil to you to serve the Lord, choose for yourselves this day whom you will serve, whether the gods

*which your fathers served that were on the other side of the
River, or the gods of the Amorites, in whose land you dwell.
But as for me and my house, we will serve the Lord.*
Joshua 24:15

II. The Message

A. God will enlarge your territory through unexpected encounters that are P_____.

*And Mordecai had brought up Hadassah, that is, Esther, his
uncle's daughter, for she had neither father nor mother.
The young woman was lovely and beautiful. When her
father and mother died, Mordecai took her as his own
daughter. So it was, when the king's command and decree
were heard, and when many young women were gathered
at Shushan the citadel, under the custody of Hegai, that
Esther also was taken to the king's palace, into the care of
Hegai the custodian of the women.* Esther 2:7-8

B. God will enlarge your territory through new opportunities that are P_____.

*Now when the turn came for Esther…to go in to the king,
she requested nothing but what Hegai the king's eunuch, the
custodian of the women advised. And Esther obtained
favor in the sight of all who saw her. So Esther was taken
to King Ahasuerus, into his royal palace. The king loved
Esther more than all the other women, and she obtained
grace and favor in his sight more than all the virgins; so he
set the royal crown upon her head and made her queen
instead of Vashti.* Esther 2:15-17

C. God will enlarge your territory through moments of influence that are P_____.

*Now when He got into a boat, His disciples followed Him.
And suddenly a great tempest arose on the sea, so that the
boat was covered with the waves. But He was asleep. Then*

His disciples came to Him and awoke Him saying, "Lord, save us! We are perishing!" But He said to them, "Why are you fearful, O you of little faith?" Then He arose and rebuked the winds and the sea. And there was a great calm. And the men marveled, saying, "Who can this be, that even the winds and the sea obey Him?."   Matthew 8:23-27

III. The Method

A. Remain faithful and flexible as you determine

God's W _____.

Then Esther told them to return this answer to Mordecai: "Go, gather all the Jews who are present in Shushan, and fast for me; neither eat nor drink for three days, night or day. My maids and I will fast likewise. And so I will go to the king, which is against the law; and if I perish, I perish." Esther 4:15-16

And the world is passing away, and the lust of it; but he who does the will of God abides forever.   1 John 2:17

B. Remain humble and honored as you discover

God's W _____.

Oh, the depth of the riches both of the wisdom and knowledge of God! How unsearchable are His judgements and His ways past finding out.   Romans 11:33

Show me Your ways, O Lord; Teach me Your paths. Lead me in Your truth and teach me, For You are the God of my salvation; On You I wait all the day.   Psalm 25:4-5

CONCLUSION
And whatever you do, do it heartily, as to the Lord and not to men, knowing that from the Lord you will receive the reward of the inheritance; for you serve the Lord Christ. Colossians 3:23-24

ENLARGE MY TERRITORY!

1. How does a woman's territory differ from that of a man? How would their territory be similar?

2. Consider the story of Joseph and talk about how God expanded his territory throughout his life. Read Genesis 50:19-20 and determine the mindset Joseph chose and how God used him to save many lives.

3. What are some areas in which a woman finds it particularly difficult to relinquish control? What does this reveal about her trust in God? What does Proverbs 3:5-6 advise us to do?

4. Why is it important to ask for expanded territory? How does being humble affect the way you determine God's will in your decisions regarding new territory?

PUT YOUR HAND ON ME!

Introduction

And Jabez called on the God of Israel saying, "Oh, that You would bless me indeed, and enlarge my territory, that Your hand would be with me, and that You would keep me from evil, that I may not cause pain!" So God granted him what he requested.   1 Chronicles 4:10

I. The Mindset

And Jabez called on the God of Israel saying, "Oh, that Your hand would be with me!" So God granted him what he requested.   1 Chronicles 4:10

A. The Hand of God involves His

S _____.

"Nevertheless I tell you the truth. It is to your advantage that I go away; for if I do not go away, the Helper will not come to you; but if I depart, I will send Him to you."   John 16:7

"But the Helper, the Holy Spirit, whom the Father will send in My name, He will teach you all things, and bring to your rememberance all things that I sais to you."   John 14:26

Therefore He who supplies the Spirit to you and works miracles among you, does He do it by the works of the law, or by the hearing of faith?   Galatians 3:5

B. The Hand of God is S _____.

And Moses said, "The people whom I am among are six hundred thousand men on foot; yet You have said, 'I will

give them meat, that they may eat for a whole month.'
Shall flocks and herds be slaughtered for them, to provide
enough for them? Or shall all the fish of the sea be
gathered together for them, to provide enough for them?"
And the Lord said to Moses, "Has the Lord's arm been
shortened? Now you shall see whether what I say will
happen to you or not."   Numbers 11:21-23

II. The Message

A. The Hand of God is needed in the

M _____.

O God, You are my God; Early will I seek You; My soul
thirsts for You; My flesh longs for You in a dry and thirsty
land where there is no water.   Psalm 63:1

I say then: walk in the Spirit, and you will not fulfill the
lusts of the flesh.   Galatians 5:16

For he who sows to his flesh will of the flesh reap
corruption, but he who sows to the Spirit will of the Spirit
reap everlasting life.   Galatians 6:8

B. The Hand of God is needed in your

M _____.

Therefore judge nothing before the time, until the Lord
comes, Who will both bring to light the hidden things of
darkness and reveal the counsels of the hearts; and then
each one's praise will come from God.   1 Corinthians 4:5

But the fruit of the Spirit is love, joy, peace, longsuffering,
kindness, goodness, faithfulness, gentleness, self-control.
Against such there is no law. And those who are Christ's
have crucified the flesh with its passions and desires. If we
live in the Spirit, let us also walk in the Spirit. Let us not
become conceited, provoking one another, envying one
another.   Galatians 5:22-26

C. The Hand of God is needed in your

M _____.

But you shall receive power when the Holy Spirit has come upon you; and you shall be witnesses to Me in Jerusalem, and in all Judea and Samaria, and to the end of the earth. Acts 1:8

This is the word of the Lord to Zerubbabel: "Not by might nor by power, but by My Spirit says the Lord of hosts." Zechariah 4:6

III. The Method

A. Choose to depend on the Hand of God

H _____.

Therefore humble yourselves under the mighty hand of God, that He may exalt you in due time. 1 Peter 5:6

For thus says the High and Lofty One who inhabits eternity, whose name is Holy: I dwell in the high and holy place, with him who has a contrite and humble spirit, to revive the spirit of the humble, and to revive the heart of the contrite ones. Isaiah 57:15

B. Choose to depend on the Hand of God

H _____.

And do not grieve the Holy Spirit of God, by whom you were sealed for the day of redemption. Let all bitterness, wrath, anger, clamor, and evil speaking be put away from you, with all malice. And be kind to one another, tender-hearted, forgiving one another, just as God in Christ also forgave you. Ephesians 4:30-32

CONCLUSION
Ah, Lord God. Behold, You have made the heavens and the earth by your great power and outstretched arm. There is nothing too hard for You. Jeremiah 32:17

PUT YOUR HAND ON ME!

1. How do most women feel about intimacy? What does
   Psalm 16:11 reveal about God's desire for intimacy
   with us?

2. Why are we commanded in Galatians 5:16 to "walk in
   the Spirit"? Name three women you know whose lives
   demonstrate the "fruit of the Spirit". What are some of
   the words others use in describing their character?

3. How will a woman's responses in life be different
   when she asks for God's hand to be with her? Read
   2 Chronicles 16:9 and discuss why God wants to
   "show Himself strong"?

4. What lies are we as women believing when we choose
   to be independent rather than dependent on God?
   Discuss John 12:24-25 and how God's Spirit is needed
   in every area of life.

KEEP ME FROM EVIL!

Introduction

"And Jabez called on the God of Israel saying, "Oh, that You would bless me indeed, and enlarge my territory, that Your hand would be with me, and that You would keep me from evil, that I may not cause pain!" So God granted him what he requested." 1 Chronicles 4:10

I. The Mindset

And Jabez called on the God of Israel saying, "Oh, that you would keep me from evil, that I may not cause pain!" So God granted him what he requested. 1 Chronicles 4:10

A. God will protect you from evil that is

I _____.

Be sober, be vigilant; because your adversary the devil walks about like a roaring lion, seeking whom he may devour. 1 Peter 5:8

B. God will use evil for your I _____.

For we do not wrestle against flesh and blood, but against principalities, against powers, against the rulers of the darkness of this age, against spiritual hosts of wickedness in the heavenly places.   Ephesians 6:12

Blessed is the man who endures temptation; for when he has been proved, he will receive the crown of life which the Lord has promised to those who love Him.   James 1:12

II. The Message

A. Keep me from evil as I resist the temptation of the T _____.

But no man can tame the tongue. It is an unruly evil; full of deadly poison. With it we bless our God and Father, and with it we curse men, who have been made in the likeness of God.   James 3:8-9

But I say to you that for every idle word man may speak, they will give account of it in the day of judgment. For by your words you will be justified, and by your words you will be condemned.   Matthew 12:36-37

Let no corrupt communication proceed out of your mouth, but what is good for necessary edification, that it may impart grace to the hearers.   Ephesians 4:29

B. Keep me from evil as I resist the temptation of the T _____.

As for you, my son Solomon, know the God of your father,
and serve Him with a loyal heart and with a willing mind;
for the Lord searches all hearts and understands all the
intent of the thoughts. If you seek Him, He will be found
by you; but if you forsake Him, He will cast you off forever.
1 Chronicles 28:8

"For My thoughts are not your thoughts, nor are your ways
My ways," says the Lord.   Isaiah 55:8

"Love your enemies, bless them who curse you, do good to
those who hate you, and pray for those who spitefully use
you and persecute you."   Matthew 5:44

Casting down arguments and every high thing that exalts
itself against the knowledge of God, bringing every thought
into captivity to the obedience of Christ.
2 Corinthians 10:5

C. Keep me from evil as I resist the temptation

of T_____.

Do all things without murmuring and disputing.
Philippians 2:14

In everything give thanks; for this is the will of God in
Christ Jesus for you.   1 Thessalonians 5:18

But godliness with contentment is great gain.
1 Timothy 6:6

III. The Method

A. Face your enemy C _____.

Lest Satan should take advantage of us, for we are not ignorant of his devices.   2 Corinthians 2:11

Therefore submit to God. Resist the devil and he will flee from you.   James 4:7

Yet Michael the archangel, in contending with the devil, when he disputed about the body of Moses, dared not bring against him a reviling accusation, but said, "The Lord rebuke you!"   Jude 1:9

B. Follow your God C _____.

Finally, my brethren, be strong in the Lord and in the power of His might.   Ephesians 6:10

But the people who know their God shall be strong, and carry out great exploits.   Daniel 11:32b

But the Lord is faithful who will establish you and guard you from the evil one.   2 Thessalonians 3:3

CONCLUSION

And the Lord will deliver me from every evil work, and preserve me for His heavenly kingdom. To Him be glory forever and ever. Amen!   2 Timothy 4:18

KEEP ME FROM EVIL!

1. What are some specific temptations that women face during the course of a day? How can these temptations be avoided?

2. How have you seen God use evil in someone's life for good? Read 1 John 5:4 and discuss how faith makes a difference.

3. Why do we need God to keep evil away from us? How often do we pray this way?

4. What are some obvious devices the enemy will use against a woman to tempt her to fall into sin? What does 2 Thessalonians 3:3 promise us?

THE
PRAYER of JABEZ
for Women

LEADER'S
GUIDE

SESSION *1* BLESS ME INDEED!

*J*abez called on the God of Israel saying, "Oh, that You would bless me indeed, and enlarge my territory, that Your hand would be with me, and that You would keep me from evil, that I may not cause pain!" So God granted him what he requested.
1 Chronicles 4:10

Introduction. Read the above verse and introduce the concept of today's session, God's blessing.

God wants to bless you. It's a statement that makes us uncomfortable, maybe even a little guilty. With so many people in the world in need, why should God give us more? But God's concept of blessing goes beyond material things and to the cries of our hearts. He is the only One who understands and hears that cry. He is the only One who can bless your life because He's our Creator.

The Video. Allow 30 minutes for the video presentation. Encourage your group to follow along in their workbooks.

A Woman's Guide to Jabez. Use these questions to get your group talking about the video they just saw.

1. Have you prayed for God to bless you in the past? If so, what happened?

2. Many of us come to God with a specific agenda in mind, something we're already doing that we want God to bless. Have you ever asked God to bless you in the way He chooses? If not, why?

3. What is at the root of our reluctance to place our entire life including our goals and daily schedules-in God's hands to do with as He chooses?

4. As mentioned in the video, God wants us to give Him the recognition for the blessings in our lives. Take a few minutes at the close of this session and acknowledge the blessings God has placed in your life.

Darlene's Challenge. End the group session re-emphasizing Darlene's challenge at the end of the video to ask God to bless you in a His own unique way. Read Psalm 139 aloud.

SESSION 2 ENLARGE MY TERRITORY!

*J*abez called on the God of Israel saying, "Oh, that You would bless me indeed, and enlarge my territory, that Your hand would be with me, and that You would keep me from evil, that I may not cause pain!" So God granted him what he requested.

1 Chronicles 4:10

Introduction. Read the above verse and introduce the concept of today's session, enlarging your territory.

How many of you would like to have more things to do? Many of us live for moments of freedom from our stressful schedules. But what if God set your agenda every day? What if you dared to pray that He enlarge your territory-making your daily routine more significant by allowing Him to use you to impact others? Today we're going to find out what happens when we dare to ask God to infuse the mundane things in our life with Him.

The Video. Allow 30 minutes for the video presentation. Encourage your group to follow along in their workbooks.

A Woman's Guide to Jabez. Use these questions to get your group talking about the video they just saw.

1. What does your territory look like?

2. How many of you are reluctant to pray this part of the prayer in fear that your life will be more stressful than it already is?

3. Think about what you did yesterday. If you had asked God to let you do more for Him, what opportunities do you think you could have had within your daily routine?

Darlene's Challenge. End the group session re-emphasizing Darlene's challenge at the end of the video to ask God to enlarge your territory. Challenge your group to ask God to let you do more for Him. Remind your group that when God enlarges your territory, you gain ground, not lose it. And it's God's job to enlarge your territory, not yours. Our job is to be obedient to Him.

SESSION 3 PUT YOUR HAND ON ME!

*J*abez called on the God of Israel saying, "Oh, that You
would bless me indeed, and enlarge my territory, that Your
hand would be with me, and that You would keep me from
evil, that I may not cause pain!" So God granted him what he
requested.

1 Chronicles 4:10

Introduction. Read the above verse and introduce the concept of today's session, place Your hand upon me.

God desires to work through your life to accomplish His blessing and the new opportunities He gives us to serve Him. But He doesn't expect us to do it alone. Today, we'll find out what happens when we ask God to strengthen us with His Spirit.

The Video. Allow 30 minutes for the video presentation. Encourage your group to follow along in their workbooks.

A Woman's Guide to Jabez. Use these questions to get your group talking about the video they just saw.

1. Have you ever tried to do something and you knew that while you had planned well for the task, you had forgotten to prepare spiritually? Explain.

2. Each of us faces a limit of our own resources and abilities. Despite the image of strong, independent women our culture projects, God wants us to be dependent on Him. In what areas of your life do you find it difficult to relinquish control to God?

3. One woman starts out the day praying and reading her Bible. The other starts her day with the alarm clock. Who has done both? What is the difference?

Darlene's Challenge. End the group session re-emphasizing Darlene's challenge at the end of the video to ask God to place His hand on you. Remind your group that God stretches us with the situations we encounter daily. Life will be beyond what we can endure on it, yet God promises to always be with us.

SESSION 4 KEEP ME FROM EVIL!

*J*abez called on the God of Israel saying, "Oh, that You would bless me indeed, and enlarge my territory, that Your hand would be with me, and that You would keep me from evil, that I may not cause pain!" So God granted him what he requested.

1 Chronicles 4:10

Introduction. Read the above verse and introduce the concept of today's session, God's blessing.

September 11, 2001 was a painful reminder that the world is not a peaceful place. Our country experienced violence and terror firsthand, not just a story tucked away in the international part of the news. But Christians are in war daily—spiritually. Today, we will look at the ways God protects us from evil. We still will go through bad things in our life, but God will shield us and give us peace through life's storms.

The Video. Allow 30 minutes for the video presentation. Encourage your group to follow along in their workbooks.

A Woman's Guide to Jabez. Use these questions to get your group talking about the video they just saw.

1. Of the three temptations in the video—the tongue, thoughts, and thanklessness—which do you struggle with the most?

2. What are some additional temptations women face? How are they different from men?

3. Have you been aware of any spiritual battles in your own life? Explain.

Darlene's Challenge. End the group session re-emphasizing Darlene's challenge at the end of the video to ask God to keep you from evil. Read through the armor of God this week, Ephesians 6:10-18. Encourage your group also to pray the entire pray every day for 30 days, not just repeating the words, but remembering the principles behind each particular part of Jabez's prayer.